THE RED SOX FAN'S
LITTLE BOOK OF WISDOM

BOOKS BY CURT SMITH

America's Dizzy Dean

Long Time Gone

Voices of The Game

The Red Sox Fan's Little Book of Wisdom

The Storytellers

Also Available from Diamond Communications, Inc.
THE CUBS FAN'S LITTLE BOOK OF WISDOM
by Jim Langford
THE CARDINALS FAN'S LITTLE BOOK OF WISDOM
by Rob Rains

THE RED SOX FAN'S
LITTLE BOOK OF WISDOM
A Fine Sense of the Ridiculous

by Curt Smith

Diamond Communications, Inc.
South Bend, Indiana
1994

THE RED SOX FAN'S LITTLE BOOK OF WISDOM

Copyright © 1994 by Curt Smith

Manufactured in the United States of America
10 9 8 7 6 5 4 3 2 1

DIAMOND COMMUNICATIONS, INC.
POST OFFICE BOX 88 • SOUTH BEND, INDIANA 46624
(219) 299-9278 • FAX (219) 299-9296

Library of Congress Cataloging-in-Publication Data

Smith, Curt.
    The Red Sox fan's little book of wisdom : a fine sense of the
ridiculous / by Curt Smith.
        p.   cm.
    ISBN 0-912083-76-X : $5.95
    1. Boston Red Sox (Baseball team)--Humor. 2. Boston Red Sox
(Baseball team)--Miscellanea.   I. Title.
GV875.B62S65   1994
796.357'64'09744610207--dc20   94-23541
                                                                CIP

To the memory of
Raymond and Viola Stuart

"*I have a fine sense of the ridiculous,
but no sense of humor.*"

—Edward Albee, in *Who's Afraid of Virginia Woolf?*,
    presaging Don Buddin and Matt Young

• INTRODUCTION •

Imagine two men stranded on a South Sea isle from Providence, Rhode Island, and Presque Isle, Maine. The strangers differ in age, race, religion, income, background, and career. Their common denominator is the Boston Red Sox.

One day in late 1988, I visited A. Bartlett Giamatti at his New York office. I said that I was a Nixon Republican and Red Sox fan and asked, "Does that bespeak masochism or loyalty?"

Giamatti sat back and roared his teddy bear of a laugh. "Clearly," he said, "it speaks of both."

The term *Book of Wisdom* may seem oxymoronic to the Red Sox fan. If we were wise, we would root for someone else. I beseech parents of young children not to adopt the Olde Towne Team. Life brings enough heartache as it is. Yet what evokes more love than New England's civic crucible? The Sox are grand and awful, stirring and infuriating, oft beaten and more oft self-defeating—but they are *ours*.

Like any relative, the Sox rouse a Rubik's Cube of memory. Thus, this compendium of fact, quote, and lesson. Think of it as prelude—like 1946 treking to '48-49 which led through 1967 to 1978 and '86. Reading entries, jot yours down and mail them to me (P.O. Box 88, South Bend, Indiana 46624). In the sequel, full credit and a free copy will go to the author of each entry—more than you ever got, say, from Cal Koonce or Juan Beniquez.

A Dublin ballad says, "Being Irish means laughing at life knowing that in the end life will break your heart." Ask fans in Southington, Connecticut, friends in Nashua, New Hampshire, or my mother born 40 miles from Boston. Being Irish is a lark *vs.* brooking Bob Bolin, Willard Nixon, Jerry Casale, and Willie Tasby.

—*Curt Smith*
Brookfield, Wisconsin, and Blue Hill, Maine

(Un)sad, but true.

"When I was seven years old, my father took me to
Fenway Park for the first time, and as I grew up I
knew that as a building it was on the level of Mount
Olympus, the Pyramid at Giza, the nation's capital,
the czar's Winter Palace, and the Louvre—
except, of course, that it was better than all those
inconsequential places."—A. Bartlett Giamatti, 1988

The more things change...

...the more baseball stays the same. In 1911, the
American League was trying to shorten games. One day,
Red Sox pitcher Ed Karger threw a pitch before outfielders
were ready that the A's Stuffy McInnis lined to right field.
Shades of Jim Rice: Thinking it a warmup toss, Boston outfielders
failed to run—the result, an inside-the-park home run.

Think about tomorrow.

Before Fenway Park, the Red Sox played near a site
where Bill Cody later brought his Wild West Show.
A great Boston fan-to-be, "Nuff Ced" McGreevey,
roared, "Who's going to play second base, Sitting Bull?"
He couldn't know about Pumpsie Green.

Timing is everything.

On April 16, 1912, the Sox dedicated their new home
at Landsdowne and Jersey Streets. They won its first
game on April 20—a 7-6 victory over the New York
then-Highlanders. Omen-watchers were delighted:
Fenway Park opened the week the Titanic sank.

I want a man with a slow (better, healthy) hand.

In the spring after Smokey Joe Wood's grand 1912, the 34-5 pitcher fell on his throwing hand and broke a thumb. It never healed properly. Watching movies, Joe couldn't lift his arm over the theatre seat. Fast-forward to Carly Simon: Joe hadn't "got time for the pain." Nor the Sox for Wood—released in 1915.

Worry if,
oh, say, he can't see.

Broadway producer Harry Frazee, doubling as Red Sox
owner, was the first owner to play "The Star-Spangled Banner"
before a baseball game—September 9, 1918. Let the record
show that Babe Ruth was then still a Red Sox.

7

Check what's in a name.

In 1918, Boston won its fourthWorld Series in
seven years—and fifth since the Classic began in 1903.
Appropos of everything: In '18, the first National Guard
unit arrived in France—the Twenty-sixth Division.
Its moniker was "Yankee."

Beware of overconfidence.

Perhaps the Sox used up providence in 1918.
As a part-time player, Ruth hit a league-leading
11 homers; Joe Bush won five complete-game 1-0
shutouts; pitcher Carl Mays completed 30 of 33
games he started—including both games of one
twin-bill; and third baseman Fred Thomas
played in the World Series while on special furlough
from the Navy. Maybe no luck was left.

Friendship has its limits.

In 1919, Ruth hit a big-league record 29 homers.
On January 5, 1920, Harry Frazee sold him to
New York for $300,000. He needed the money to
bankroll Broadway plays—among them, *My Lady Friends*.
Noting the sign for one Frazee production flop, one fan
said, "Well, they're the only friends the SOB has."

Bathtub gin has its place.

Ruth's sale to New York occurred 11 days before
Prohibition—ironic, since it drove fans to drink.
"You're going to ruin the Red Sox in Boston for
a long time," Sox manager Ed Barrow told
Frazee on learning of the sale. It did, and does.

Who needs *The Music Man*?

Aptly, Frazee's *My Lady Friends* was a farce.
The Red Sox had won five of baseball's first 15
World Series. After selling Babe, they finished last
in nine of the first 12 Ruthless years—and won
exactly a single pennant in the next 47 years.

12

Tiparillos don't pay the bulldog.

Ruth was not reluctant to leave The Hub.
"They had a Babe Ruth Day for me last year
and I had to buy my wife's ticket to the game,"
he told reporters in early 1920. "Fifteen
thousand fans show up and all I got was a cigar."

Fool me twice, shame on me.

On June 27, 1923, a Red Sox' pitcher
yielded 13 runs as Cleveland won, 27-3.
Frank O'Doul was released, then re-emerged
as a National League outfielder. Like Ruth, Lefty
loved his new domicile. Twice, he led the N.L.
in hitting. The Sox could have used him. In
1927, Ruth outhomered their entire *team*—60-28.

Keep No Way Out
in the VCR.

"I started at the bottom in this business, and worked my
way right into the sewer."—Art Carney. The 1925-30
Red Sox six times placed eighth in an eight-team league.
The box score: 311-603, and 292-1/2 games behind.

"Baseball is Boston's real religion." —Tip O'Neill, 1955.

Third baseman Marty McManus was attending Mass when the Red Sox named him manager in 1932. Thereafter, he had reason to attend. His teams went 95-153.

We all have fish to fry.

In 1928, rookie Ed Morris won a grand 19 of the Red Sox'
57 victories. He was a one-year flash—winning just 23
games the rest of his career before being fatally stabbed
by a jealous husband at a 1932 fish fry.

"Green Acres Is The Place To Be."

Fenway's Duffy's Cliff was a 10-foot incline named after
Red Sox left fielder George "Duffy" Lewis. It was leveled
after 1933 for a 37-foot-high "Green Monster" wall and later
a 23-foot net atop it to protect windows on the other side of
Landsdowne Street. Sadly, it couldn't protect Mike Torrez.

Call toll-free
A-r-t-h-u-r M-u-r-r-a-y.

Smead Jolley once fell down on Duffy's Cliff
while chasing a carom off the wall. He told teammates
between innings, "You smart guys taught me how to go
up the hill, but nobody taught me how to come down."

The fault lies in ourselves, not our stars.

"That left-field wall was so close that if you were a right-handed pitcher and threw sidearm, your knuckles would scrape it."—Vernon (Lefty) Gomez, scraped less than most

Know when to say "when."

In Game One of the '33 World Series, Sox
broadcaster Fred Hoey reached the NBC
Radio booth with evident breath and fumbling.
Inebriated, Hoey was quickly yanked from
the air. Explanation: he had "a bad cold." Fred
may have tried to drink off Boston's 1933—at
63-86, its 15th straight second-division finish.

Head Sox rhymes with dead flops.

On September 27, 1935, Boston trailed, 5-3, but had the bases loaded, none out, and Joe Cronin at bat. Joe lined a ball that glanced off Indians' third baseman Odell Hale's head. It caromed on the fly to shortstop Billy Knickerbocker, who threw to Roy Hughes on second base for the second out. Hughes then threw to first—tripling Mel Almada—to complete a *true* no-brainer.

Imagine Jeffrey MacDonald as Skipper.

Boston's "Fatal Vision" sold Babe Ruth to New York,
spurned Pie Traynor in a tryout, shipped Bucky Walters
to the Phillies, traded Red Ruffing for Cedric Durst,
peddled Pee Wee Reese to Brooklyn, passed on
signing Jackie Robinson, and later sent Jeff Bagwell
to Houston. The Sox did, however,
ink Ted Lepcio to a 1952-59 contract.

Know (or change?) thyself.

Players traded to New York were said to perform
better in Yankees' pinstripes. Away from Boston, even
a new name helped. Pete Jablonowski pitched horribly
for the 1932 Red Sox. Renamed Pete Appleton,
he was 14-6 for Washington in 1936.

Welcome *Something Wonderful.*

Born in San Diego exactly 12 days before the Sox
won their last World Series, a rookie stood
next to Bobby Doerr in 1938 spring training. Doerr said,
"Wait 'till you see Jimmie Foxx hit." Replied Ted Williams:
"Wait 'till Foxx sees *me* hit."

These bats are made for walkin'.

On June 16, 1938, Jimmie Foxx became the only A.L. player to draw six walks in a nine-inning game. By dint of contrast, center fielder Doc Cramer hit .302 in 3,111 Red Sox' at-bats—yet smacked only one home run.

Don't worry, be happy.

Ted Williams struck out in his first two major
league at-bats in 1939. Ahead, two Triple Crowns
(1942 and '47), six batting titles, and his Everest
.406 of 1941—and a niche as John Wayne in
baseball woolies for a generation of Americans.

27

Let's play, "What's My Line?"

Williams, Carl Yastrzemski, Jim Rice, and
Mike Greenwell all became Sox All-Star left fielders.
Name the fifth man: Good luck.
Unsung Bob Johnson, 37, in 1944 while
The Kid was in the Marines.

Birds of a feather...

In 1945, the A's Hal Peck made a bad throw
that hit a Fenway pigeon and deflected to the
second baseman. The pigeon was killed, and
Sox runner Skeeter Newsome was tagged out.
That same year, Boston outfielder Tom McBride
camped under what he thought was a long belt by
Sam Chapman. Too late, he found it was a pigeon.

...Do flock together.

Like Sox pitching, Fenway pigeons beware.
The Browns' Billy Hunter once hit a pigeon
in batting practice. In 1974, Willie Horton hit
a foul pop which skulled a bird. Ted Williams
couldn't stand them—using a rifle until, unlike
A.L. hurlers, the Humane Society stopped him.

Earning his keep.

Like many players, 1941-46 Red Sox reliever Mike Ryba played a different position in each inning of a minor-league game—and more. At game's end, he drove the team bus to the train.

"For better or worse..."

unites Red Sox fans. Winning 104 games, the
1946 club had little need for a bullpen. So Mr. Ryba
focused instead on hotel lobby-sitting. In one
month, he counted 35 weddings.

Teddy Ballgame (the good).

On September 13, 1946, Boston clinched the
A.L. flag by beating Cleveland, 1-0, on Ted's
only inside-the-park homer. In Game Three
of the World Series, St. Louis manager Eddie Dyer
left only one player on the left side of the
diamond—the Williams Shift. The next day,
a headline blared, "Williams Bunts!"

Teddy Ballgame (the bad).

In inning eight, Game Seven, of the '46 Series,
the score was 3-all when Enos Slaughter scored
from first base on Harry Walker's double to give
St. Louis a 4-3 victory. Boarding the train for
return home to Boston, Ted forgot to close the blinds.
More than a thousand fans saw him weep in his
compartment. The reason—a .200 Series average
for the greatest hitter who ever lived.

Himself (the ugly).

Williams was many things—but not a pitcher.
On August 24, 1940, tired of Ted's boasting,
manager Joe Cronin put him in for the last
two innings of a 12-1 loss to Detroit. Ted gave
up three hits and one run—and struck out Rudy York
on a called strike 3. Underwhelmed by Williams'
prowess, the Sox never pitched him again.

Have a sense of humor.

Philadelphian by birth and Victorian by bearing,
Joe McCarthy became manager in 1948.
How would he treat Williams' spurning team
rules by refusing to wear a necktie? Comically.
Marse Joe appeared at a hotel in spring training
in an open-necked sports shirt. "Anyone," he said,
"who can't get along with a .400 hitter is crazy."

Before "Bonanza."

On July 4, 1948, Williams staged a pre-television repeat—
becoming the first batter to ever face the same
pitcher three times in a single inning.

37

Good karma doesn't last forever.

The Sox dropped a playoff for the '48 pennant.
Next, 1949—how could this ballclub *lose?* Four
regulars batted more than .300. Williams and
Vern Stephens each knocked in 150-plus runs.
Dom DiMaggio hit safely in 34 straight games.
Mel Parnell and Ellis Kinder, winning 48 games,
were baseball's best pitchers. It seemed so easy—
'till a season-ending weekend in New York.

Damn Yankees.

On October 2, 1949, the Yankees and Sox
met to decide the A.L. pennant. Trailing, 1-0,
in the eighth inning, McCarthy pinch-hit for starter
Kinder. In the bottom half, the Yankees scored four
runs and won, 5-3. The two fought on the train back
to New York, and each sought a flask. Said one
teammate, "Ellie could drink more bourbon and
pitch more clutch baseball than anyone I ever knew."

39

Where have you gone, Cornelius McGillicuddy?

Connie Mack called pitching 90 percent of baseball—
e.g., the '50 Sox. Seven regulars batted over .300.
Rookie Walt Dropo hit 34 homers, and tied teammate
Vern Stephens with 144 RBI. Doerr had 120 RBI.
Billy Goodman led the league with a .354 average.
On June 7-8, Boston made the Browns black and
blue—winning 20-4 and 29-4. The kicker:
Boston hit .302 and finished third!

40

The longest day(s).

On July 12-13, 1951, the Red Sox and White Sox
toured the land of the Midnight Sun. The first night was
a doubleheader. Game One went the normal nine innings.
Game Two lasted 17—and Ellis Kinder threw 10 scoreless relief
innings as the Red Sox won, 5-4. A day later, Boston's Mickey
McDermott pitched the first 17 innings as Chicago won, 5-4,
in 19 innings. No hurler was paid by the pitch.

Foretelling Roseanne.

One day, the Sox' 1950-58 center fielder Jim Piersall
pretended he was a pig while leading off first base.
It so rattled Satchel Paige that the Browns'
Ancient Mariner loaded the bases and gave up a
grand-slam homer to Sammy White.

Marcus Welby,
phone your office.

Each Opening Day as president, Dwight Eisenhower
threw out a first ball which players scurried to retrieve.
One year Boston opened at Griffith Stadium. Once
hospitalized for manic depression, Piersall waited 'till
Ike tossed the ball and gave him another as players
fought for the souvenir. "Mr. President," he said, "would
you sign *this* ball while those idiots scramble for *that* one?"

A prophet without title.

In 1954, Williams hit a league-high .345 but had just
386 official plate appearances (plus 136 walks). A
batter then had to have a total of 477 official plate
appearances to qualify. The injustice made the rules
committee effect a change from official times at-bat
to plate appearances. Better late than never—
but not for No. 9, losing to Bobby Avila's .341.

Ward, make sure the Beaver washed.

A Gallup Poll says more Americans would rather relive the 1950s than any decade of the Twentieth Century. Sox fans might disagree. In eight of the 1950s' 10 years, Boston finished third ('50-1-7-8-) or fourth ('53-4-5-6).

Leave 'em laughing.

On August 7, 1956, Williams was booed for
muffing a flyball, later spat at fans as he neared
the dugout, entered it, came out, and let fly again.
Owner Tom Yawkey fined him $5,000. The next
night, Williams bombed a long home run.
Nearing the dugout—what a quipster—
he whimsically put his hand over his mouth.

The Symbol.

Of Boston's more than 1,200 players, none embodied
ineptitude more than 1956 and '58-61 shortstop
Don Buddin. Some said that Don's license plate should
read, "E-6." Others said he had no license to play.

For No. 9, a one and a two.

In 1957, baseball's Lawrence Welk shunned Geritol to bat .388—the bigs' best since 1941. Williams hit 38 homers (one for every 11 official at-bats) and had a .731 slugging percentage. Only Ted could mix Champagne Music and Narragansett Beer.

Let me make this perfectly clear.

For Sox fans hoping for a new era, this Nixon
was not the one. From 1950-58, pitcher Willard Nixon
won 69, lost 72, and had a 4.39 ERA. (He did lead A.L.
pitchers in '57 batting average—.293.) Nor was 1960-65
and '68 catcher Russ Nixon of the .256 Sox' average.
Maybe they explain why Thoroughly Modern
Milhous three times lost Massachusetts.

Was "Ramblin' Man" dedicated to No. 5?

Let America have Van Johnson. New England had Jackie Jensen. Beantown's towhead led the A.L. in run production the second half of the '50s. Jensen had five 100-plus RBI years with Boston and was voted 1958 A.L. MVP—then retired in 1960 because he hated plane travel. A year later, he returned for a last act before leaving baseball for good—by train.

Was Judy Collins a Red Sox fan?

In 1958, Williams showed his "Both Sides Now."
He threw a bat which struck a fan in the face—
ironically, Gladys Heffernan, housekeeper of Sox
general manager Joe Cronin. That Christmas, Ted
sent her a peace offering—a $500 diamond watch.
He also celebrated his sixth and final batting title—
at 40, hitting .328, the oldest man to win a title.

Be grateful for small things.

On July 21, 1959, infielder Elijah "Pumpsie" Green
broke into the Sox' lineup—ending Boston's cachet
as baseball's last all-white team. Other first black players:
The Dodgers' Jackie Robinson, the Indians' Larry Doby,
and the Cubs' Ernie Banks.
By contrast, Green hit .246 for the Red Sox.

Save the best for last.

On September 28, 1960, Williams retired as only
a Deity could—a home run, No. 521, in his final at-bat.
The next morning a Boston writer cried, "What are we
going to write about now?" On his last homer, Ted still
refused to tip his cap. Later, John Updike explained why:
"God does not answer letters."

To Heaven and back.

Carroll Hardy was the only man to pinch-hit
for Ted Williams (September 21, 1960) and
Carl Yastrzemski (May 31, 1961). The outcome:
Respectively, a double play, single, and a
changing of the guard.

"The meek shall inherit the Earth…"

…but not the American League. In July 1962, pitcher Gene Conley tried to convince Pumpsie Green to leave the Sox and go to Israel. They got off the team bus in New York and went to the airport—where Conley bought a ticket for Tel Aviv. Providence then intervened. Both returned to the Sox to preach their Gospel of Mediocrity.

Dr. Strangeglove.

The only people Dick Stuart terrorized more than
rival pitchers were Sox fans and managers. One day,
Stu got a standing ovation for picking up a wind-blown
hot dog wrapper without dropping it. "Dick was 10
years too soon with Boston," said his 1963-64 skipper,
Johnny Pesky. "He would have been a great DH."

Far from the Madding Crowd.

On September 16, 1965, Dave Morehead
pitched a weekday afternoon no-hitter before
1,247 fans at Fenway Park. The Sox drew
only 652,201 all year—461 for a September 28
game against the Angels. A cause: Boston
lost 100 games for the first time since 1932.

Always take a paddle.

"I feel myself being drawn to television like a man in a canoe heading toward Niagara Falls."—Robert Young, 1953. The longer announcer Curt Gowdy stayed at Fenway Park (1951-65), the worse the Sox got. By five-year intervals: 400-369, 385-385, and a dreary 362-445. "For the record," Gowdy laughs, "I deny any cause and effect."

58

Youth wasn't wasted on this young.

On April 18, 1964, at 19, Tony Conigliaro wafted
the first pitch ever thrown him at Fenway for a home run.
In 1965, he became the youngest-ever American League
home-run champ—'67, at 22, the youngest A.L. player
to hit 100 career homers. Next stop: Cooperstown—
until Jack Hamilton began his windup.

59

Pinch yourself—
you still won't believe it.

In 1967, Vegas dubbed the sad-sack Sox—ninth in '66—
100-1 to win the pennant. Rookie manager Dick Williams
said, "We'll win more than we lose." By July, he said, simply,
"We'll win." On the final day, Boston won the flag to transport
New England and complete The Impossible Dream. Gushed
Tom Yawkey on the night of the pennant-winning: "I haven't
had a drink in four years, but I'll have one now."
Millions still drink to *him*.

Me like 'em outcome.

One of Williams' first acts as manager was to
let/make Carl Yastrzemski step down as captain.
"We'll have only one chief—all the rest are Indians."
Yaz found a better way to lead—.326, 44 homers,
126 RBI, and Triple Crown. Said catcher Russ Gibson of
The Great One: "Nobody'd ever had a season like
Yaz in '67. Nobody"—and nobody ever has.

Hitting well is the best revenge.

In 1967, White Sox manager Eddie Stanky
called Yaz "a great ballplayer from the neck down."
No. 8 then went 6 for 9 in a doubleheader against the
White Sox—including a home run. Concluding his trot
around the bases, Yaz tipped his cap to the Brat.
Blue, it contrasted with Stanky's red face.

Tunnel vision can be 20/20.

Reggie Smith led off one '67 10th inning with
a triple and later scored—but not before hundreds
of cars backed up as a man refused to drive through
a Boston tunnel until he heard the outcome.
Many didn't mind: Outside the tunnel
their AM radios caught every pitch.

Fenway Park = Fellowship Hall.

"Karl Marx, who said religion was the [people's] opiate, would have revised himself had he watched the Red Sox unite to throw off their ninth-place chains," said the *Boston Globe*'s Bud Collins about the '67 Sox. "The Red Sox are the opiate right now, Karl, baby, although you might classify them as a religion."

There you go again.

In late '67, bad luck reclaimed the Sox. On a
California mountain near Lake Tahoe, two days
before Christmas, Cy Young Award winner
Jim Lonborg fell while skiing and tore a pair of
ligaments in his left knee. Like Joe Wood,
Frank Baumann, and Jose Santiago—Gentleman
Jim was never the same. By dint of irony, pitchers'
legs/arms have been Boston's Achilles' heel.

Déjà vu can strike all over again.

Before the 1972 season, Danny Cater was traded to Boston for reliever Sparky Lyle. That year Cater had 39 RBI—Lyle, a league-leading 35 saves. Ultimately, Sparky won a Cy Young Award—Cater, a trip to oblivion. Twice burned (i.e., Babe Ruth), the Sox became shy: No Yankees' trade for the next 14 years.

Speed kills.

Sox' timing can astound. On October 2, 1972,
the Sox and Tigers started a three-game series to
decide the A.L. East flag. Luis Aparicio was on first
when Yaz lashed a long third-inning drive to center
field at Tiger Stadium—sure to score the best runner
of our time. Ripley wouldn't believe how Little Looie
proceeded to fall down rounding third, retreat to the bag,
and find Yaz there, too. The rally, and pennant, died.

67

Hail to something old...

Richard Nixon said of The Great Wall of China,
"This *is* a great wall." Ibid, the most famed concrete
east of Beijing. Thomas Austin Yawkey died
July 9, 1976. Fenway's left-field Wall still flaunts
his and Jean Yawkey's initials in Morse Code
dot-dashed on the green expanse near the scoreboard.

...and something new.

Yawkey padded the outfield wall in 1976 after
rookie Fred Lynn crashed into it in the '75 World Series.
Lynn was the only freshman to ever win the MVP
Award (.331 average, 21 homers, and 105 RBI),
and seemed headed for Cooperstown. Maybe he
should have requested a Triple-A Triptik.

(69)

But Edward G. Robinson loved the Dodgers.

At 12:34 A.M. October 22, 1975, Carlton Fisk hit a 12th-inning Series homer to win Game Six, 7-6, *vs.* Cincinnati—but how did NBC get the reaction shot of Fisk using hand signals and body English to force/pray the ball fair? Inside The Wall sat cameraman Lou Gerard— his task, follow the ball. As Fisk swung he saw a rat four feet away: "I didn't dare move, which is what I had to do to shift the viewfinder." Lou kept the lens on Fisk. The result of "You dirty rat" changed the future of TV sports.

70

Weigh what you say before you say it.

Then say it. "If you don't bear down all the time and don't have your act together, Fenway Park will bite you, eat you up, and spit you out," said 1969-78 Sox pitcher Bill Lee. Is that why he called Don Zimmer "The Gerbil"?

71

You'll like the movie more.

Nineteen seventy-eight was not *My Favorite Year*. On
July 19, the Sox were 62-28 and led the Yankees by 14 games.
Boston then lost 9 of 10—and 14 of 16 after August 29
including four straight September 7-10 to New York:
The Sox were outscored, 42-9, ergo, "The Boston Massacre."
It was a hint, as they say, of things to come.

72

"Be yourself" is usually good advice.

Unless you're Don Zimmer. As Sox 1976-80 manager,
he was a great third-base coach. After losing the
"Massacre's" first three games, Yaz begged Zim to start
Bill Lee. Hating Lee, Zimmer chose another lefty—rookie
Bobby Sprowl—repeating, "The kid's got ice water in his
veins." Sprowl didn't last an inning, and never threw
another pitch in a Red Sox uniform. Maybe it was tap.

Wendell Willkie was correct.

We *are* "One World." In Rome, the late Archbishop
Humberto Medeiros used a recess of the College
of Cardinals in late 1978 to ask a Boston television
journalist how the Red Sox were doing. When Pope
John Paul I died that year, a Boston TV station teased its
upcoming newscast, "Pope Dies, Sox Still Alive."
The Pope had never heard of Bucky Dent.

A stiff breeze can spawn stiffer drinks.

On October 2, 1978, the Yankees and Red Sox met at
Fenway in a one-game playoff—prize, the A.L. East.
For most of the game, the wind had blown in from
left field. As Bucky Dent hit in the seventh inning,
Boston ahead, 2-0, it began to swirl out. Inheriting
the wind, Dent's simple fly became a three-run homer.
Final score: Yankees, 5-4.

(75)

It is better to have swung and missed...

...than never to have swung at all. In the seventh inning, Zimmer sent once-slugging Bob Bailey to pinch-hit against Goose Gossage. A fastball hitter, Bailey never took the bat off his shoulder *vs.* three Goose fastball strikes. In New England, perhaps "No-standing" zones should be renamed "No-Bailey."

Fiddler's 'Tradition' was better.

After Dent's homer, a New Haven bar owner moaned, "They [Sox] killed our fathers and now the sons of bitches are coming to get us."

77

Be grateful for (un)small things.

Lost in Dent's thunderclap was Jim Rice's Great Year:
MVP, 46 homers, 139 RBI, and 406 total bases in a
major-league record 163 games—the only A.L. player
to exceed the 400 mark in the last 55 years.

78

Like "Maggie May," "Yastrzemski Song" is a classic.

In 1989, hundreds at Cooperstown sang Jess Cain's '67 aria.
Yaz won 1969-71 Gold Gloves in left field—leading the
league in assists each year. He went to first base for five years—
then in '77 returned to outfield an errorless 140 games, lead
the league in assists again, and win his last Gold Glove. Yaz holds
A.L. records for at-bats (11,988), plate appearances (13,992),
intentional walks (190), and games (3,308). All together, class:
"He's the idol of Boston, Mass."

79

"The Man They Call Yaz" ain't mere lyrics.

After 1967, No. 8 was named president of the Arnold Bread Sportsmanship Club. Among its rules: "Success in sports— and in life—is spelled 'hard work.' " In '79, Yaz became the only A.L. player to get his 400th homer and 3,000th hit. In 1982, another feat—at 43, the oldest man to play center field. Yaz ended his career where it began—playing his first game of 1983 (in its last game) in the shadow of The (left-field) Wall.

"That Old Black Magic" ain't just a tune.

The retired numbers worn by Ted Williams (9), Joe Cronin (4), Bobby Doerr (1), and Carl Yastrzemski (8) hang on the facade overhanging right field at Fenway. What irony hath Red Sox spooks: The epigram—9/4/18—recalls the exact week the Sox won their last World Series.

Here's to the old math.

In 1983, Cleveland scored twice in the eighth inning
to take a 3-2 lead. Said Sox announcer Ken Coleman:
"Here comes the tying run and the winning run, and the
Indians win." He looked at the mound and saw Bob Stanley
standing there. "It was then," Coleman said, "that I realized
I'd goofed. Baseball is a nine, not eight, inning game."

What would they hit today?

On May 1, 1982, the Sox held their first Old-Timers' Day.
The outfield: Ted Williams (63), Jimmy Piersall (53), and
Jackie Jensen (55). Said a writer, "Lloyd's of London couldn't
insure what their salaries would command today."

Maybe they were watching...

the Williams-Piersall-Jensen trio. In 1983, Jim Rice
homered three times in a game *vs.* Toronto—six years
to the day (August 29) after he did the same *vs.* Oakland.
Dwight Evans was the only A.L. player to hit 20 or
more home runs each year from 1981 through '89.

London can't match this fog.

Dennis "Oil Can" Boyd was a talented 1982-89 pitcher
who was a bit, shall we say, on the blockhead side. One
day a Sox game was postponed in Cleveland as fog
rolled off Lake Erie. "That's what you get,"
said The Can, "when you build a stadium on the ocean."

Did Wade Boggs like "Highway Patrol"?

"If you don't have a girl on the show, you don't have
to shave so often."—Broderick Crawford, 1956.
Wade outlasted Margo Adams' show/telling all about
their extramarital affair to record baseball's most-ever
(seven in 1983-89) straight seasons of 200 or more hits.

These are the good old days.

"In the '50s," said former Voice Ned Martin,
"the Red Sox had great players cursed by mediocre
clubs." In 1985, Wade Boggs had a club-record 240 hits
(bigs' most since 1930) to hit .368 for the batting title—
Boston's highest since Williams' .388 in '57. He hit safely
in 135 games to tie a big-league mark—187 singles set a
Sox' record—and 758 plate appearances were an A.L. high.
So what? Boston finished 81-81.
Norm Zauchin would understand.

CONTROL works—not KAOS.

In the 1980s, Roger Clemens recorded 38 double-figure strikeout games. No other Sox pitcher had more than 18 (Smokey Joe Wood.) Maxwell Smart would have rejoiced April 29, 1986. Clemens set a big-league record by striking out 20 Mariners—including a league-tying eight straight. "Chief, would you believe? Not a single walk."

KAOS works, too.

One day in May 1986, the Red Sox got 13 walks—
but no one scored. In the 10th inning, Boston trailed
by a run as Steve Lyons and Marty Barrett slid into
second base from different directions. Stunned, outfielder
George Wright threw the ball into the Texas dugout.
Both walked home—as the Olde Towne Team won.

And away we go!—Jackie Gleason

On April 7, 1986, in baseball's season opener, off
Detroit's Jack Morris, Dwight Evans hit the first pitch
of the year for a homer at Tiger Stadium. It had never
happened before—or since—in major-league
history. "How Sweet It Was!"—and remained, 'till
Game Six of the '86 World Series.

He who laughs last, laughs best.

With two outs, no Mets on base, and Boston leading Game Six, 5-3, in the bottom of the 10th inning—the Yawkeys on their feet in the dugout, the Shea Stadium message board prematurely blazing, "Congratulations Red Sox," and Boston twice a single strike from victory—Bruce Hurst already picked the Classic's MVP and the Series trophy in the Sox' clubhouse— well, you know the rest. Whose fault? Ours—for not recalling the Red Sox as baseball's Heartbreak Kids.

Forget love and marriage.

Bob Stanley and Bill Buckner go together like
a horse and carriage. Game Six linked them then
and now. Steamer's wild pitch plated the Mets' tying
run—Billy Buck's error the winner on Mookie Wilson's
dribbler. Fans remembered. Once, spotting Stanley, a
Boston driver literally rammed Bob's car. Buckner finally
moved back west to shake the ridicule. Ignore Laurel and
Hardy. In New England, sad-sack means another team.

The macabre has a certain appeal.

In 1987, Joel Krakow of the Captain Video Store unwrapped a shipment that included the World Series' '86 highlight film. Recalling Game Six, he knew where to place the baseball tape—the horror/science fiction section of his West Newton, MA, store.

You only make one first impression.

On April 4, 1988, newly-acquired reliever Lee Smith yielded a 10th-inning homer to Alan Trammell as the Sox lost their home opener. Seeing it all before, the *Boston Herald* bannered: "Wait 'Till Next Year." We have, and are.

Don't let a bad day (or team) discourage you.

Dick Radatz worked a franchise-high 79 games for the tawdry '64 Red Sox. Jeff Reardon saved a record 40 games in 1991. On the other hand, Earl Wilson apparently didn't trust his infield to touch the ball. In 1964, he yielded a franchise-most 37 home runs.

Long ball 101 was full.

On April 19, 1994, Mo Vaughn and Tim Naehring
twice hit back-to-back homers as the Sox beat
Oakland, 13-5. "Yes, the ball's been flying around
the ballpark," Naehring said. "But whether it's juiced
or not, I don't know. I missed that class in college."

Mr. Wizard.

In 1994, the majors hit a record number of home runs—
or would have, had a strike not intervened. Mo Vaughn
said he knew the reason—"Because we're hitting them hard."
Not hard enough to avoid a second-division finish.

Silver lining.

On April 12, 1994, Scott Cooper hit for the cycle as
Boston beat Kansas City, 22-11, the most runs allowed
in Royals' history. "Yeah, it's a little humiliating,"
said Kansas City catcher Mike Macfarlane, "but you've
got to look at the positive side. We scored 11."

You take Manhattan.

Through 1994, the Red Sox had won more games
than lost *vs.* the Orioles, Angels, White Sox, Tigers,
Brewers, A's, Mariners, Rangers, and Blue Jays.
Boston was under .500 against three Middle
American teams—Indians, Royals, and Twins—
and one from a foreign City-State—New York.

Valhalla is no promised land.

Only five clubs eclipse the Red Sox' 32 inductees at
Cooperstown—three executives, six managers,
seven players who played fewer than 200 games for
Boston, and 16 who played more than 200. Who
wouldn't trade them all for the first Sox' World Series
ring in the lifetime of most fans living?

If Baptism fails, try Benediction.

"Fenway," said Bill Lee, "is a shrine where people come for religious rites." Which Testament deserves Don Zimmer? Buried in a mock '93 ceremony, The Curse of the Bambino lives.

101

Otis Campbell never went to Fenway Park.

"The funny thing is, I don't think I've ever been really drunk in my life."—Hal Smith as "The Andy Griffith Show" 's town drunk. Nineteen-forty-six, 1948-49, 1972, 1974, 1977-78, 1986, and points before, after, and in between. Neighbor, go grab yourself a 'Gansett. Here's to New England's heirloom of the heart.

• ABOUT THE AUTHOR •

Curt Smith is an author, radio talk host, television essayist and writer, and former Presidential speechwriter. *THE RED SOX FAN'S LITTLE BOOK OF WISDOM: A Fine Sense of the Ridiculous* is his fourth book.

Smith's prior books are *America's Dizzy Dean*, *Long Time Gone*, and *Voices of The Game*. In 1994, he wrote, co-produced, and appeared in a 90-minute ESPN-TV *Voices of The Game* special, hosted by Jason Robards, Jr.—and helped write the Martin Sheen-hosted video documentary, *Once There Was A Ballpark*. Smith's next book, *The Storytellers*, will be released in May 1995 by MacMillan.

Smith hosts radio's popular "Mid-Day Milwaukee" on Milwaukee ABC affiliate WISN—and is regular guest on National Empowerment Network's TV media show and essayist on Prime Sports Channel's "Ed Randall's Talking Baseball." He writes a *Baseball America* media column and stories for *Reader's Digest* and *The Diamond*, the official chronicle of Major League Baseball.

Formerly a Gannett reporter and *The Saturday Evening Post* senior editor, Smith wrote more 1989-93 speeches than anyone for President Bush. Among them were the "Just War" Persian Gulf Address; Nixon and Reagan Library Dedication speeches; and speech aboard the *USS Arizona* on the 50th anniversary of Pearl Harbor.

Leaving the White House, Smith hosted a smash series at the Smithsonian Institution based on his acclaimed *Voices* before turning to radio and TV. Born in Caledonia, New York, he lives in Brookfield, Wisconsin, and jokes that the Stairway to Heaven favors fans of Broadway musicals, "The Andy Griffith Show," and the Boston Red Sox.